Following the Silence

Also by Marc Harshman

POETRY

Believe What You Can: Poems
Woman in Red Anorak: Poems
Green-Silver and Silent: Poems
Local Journeys
A Song for West Virginia
All That Feed Us: West Virginia Poems
Local Journeys
Rose of Sharon
Turning Out the Stones

CHILDREN'S BOOKS

The Storm
A Little Excitement
Fallingwater: The Building of Frank Lloyd Wright's Masterpiece
One Big Family
Mountain Christmas
Only One Neighborhood
Roads
Red Are the Apples
All the Way to Morning
Moving Days
Uncle James
Only One
Rocks in My Pockets
Snow Company

FOLLOWING THE SILENCE

POEMS

MARC HARSHMAN

Press 53
——•——
Winston-Salem

Press 53, LLC
PO Box 30314
Winston-Salem, NC 27130

First Edition

Cover art, "Red Road 2," Copyright © 2018 by Caroline Jennings
Used by permision of the artist

Library of Congress Control Number
2023948743

ISBN 978-1-950413-72-0

for John & Vivien Freeman

CONTENTS

ONE

TWO

THREE

ONE

"Read your own obituary notice; they say you live longer.
Gives you second wind. New lease of life."
— James Joyce, *Ulysses*

"The way memory is the ringing after a gunshot. The way
we try to remember the gunshot but can't. The way memory
gets up after someone has died and starts walking."
— Victoria Chang, *Obit*

AUGUST GHOSTS

And so perhaps they do stand just there, lost
    in the bright and shadow of goldenrod and grapevine,
    they, the dead, whom we know would return
    if only we quit trying so hard.
We had wished verisimilitude, a crisp palimpsest
    on the mirror above grandmother's bureau
    where lavender lingers, where the stain persisted
    of the water glass in which granddad's teeth rested at night.
We had expected, if not chains and moans, at least a few footfalls in the attic
    or the slam of a door like the one just now
    when the wind swept it from your hands and the dog escaped.
Or perhaps, simply, that shimmering sheet of light loosed
    unnaturally from the shadow behind the curtains—was it *that* was them?
But we expect too little when we look
    for such audible, photographic certainty.
Even if ears could tongue the other world's glossolalia, they would not speak.
Even if eyes could review every picture ever snapped,
    those trillions of snapshots—we would not find them.
But here, with afternoon advancing, a very real grouse
    busily feeding its young on the lawn, the lawn
    stretching in the heat luxuriously toward the tree line,
    here where the winds' susurrus lifts our eyes
    into an anarchy of sunshine from the dark entanglement
    of weed and brush, here we might . . .
Here we lift our eyes as if all we had to do was follow the flickering
    of the shadows the wind unleashes, as if we
    were only trying to let a color come to mind or memory.
At this precise and smallest of moments, we can let go
    and simply let them come from some place over there
    where they are more real than we ever allowed
    when we tried making them ours.
Laughable to think we ever thought we could conjure them
    using mirrors and will power, wishful thinking and magic.

I say let them be as real as the shadows
        trickling through our hands,
        like this wind through these familiar leaves,
        like lavender, like the remembered *clonk* of a set of false teeth.
See, more boldly now, the ruffed grouse advances towards us,
        holding her head high, her babies following—
        just like that we, too, may someday follow
        hungry to be seen in the sunlight for what
        we really are.

A QUESTION

Beside the iron river, the trees burn
      with the blue light of sunset.

Where the silver of an early moon
      trails its finger, a single heron
      will disappear, motionless,
      at ease in its magic.

Its kinship with the noisier, smaller birds
      seems extraordinary but we believe
      because of books and feathers.

And what do they believe?

Something as natural as this, perhaps, where
      words follow a path across a field,
      looking for food and light, shadows and home.

FOLLOWING THE SILENCE

Trying to find words, we visit the dead:
  Gone but not forgotten.
The clouds mounted overhead, serenely white
  and quiet with that quiet a lost afternoon
  in October sometimes brings.
We sat and told stories, the dead content to listen
  to our own variations on genealogies
  so similar to theirs carved on stone.
Somehow, in the gap between one sentence
  and another, between your sister
  and, perhaps, my uncle, we kissed,
  a kiss *long enough for tasting*,
  and we sat back then and pondered.
Bemused, pleased, curious—I don't think we knew,
  nor do we now.
We embraced two giant red spruce, studied
  the orange fungus at their feet,
  listened to the forest, its crickets
  and frogs and birds, followed paths
  not knowing what we were following,
  much as our words chased after
  each other with the ease of old friends
  not knowing, nor caring where they led
  but enjoying the chase.
We sat by a stream and filled the air
  with stories about listening
  and then listened ourselves
  to the stream, listened
  to follow the silence home to our hearts.

HOW THE ENDING BEGINS

I am / unexpectedly alone in West Virginia. —Jack Gilbert

The hay barn above the river slowly settles
        among berry brambles and multi-flora rose.
Elmer said it's a quiet death most insures a secure,
        untroubled rest.
Immaculate clouds are building storms in the west
        even as the single hawk
        continues its canvass of prey.
The squirrel reconsiders his mad dance, the erratic
        map of his autumn planting of walnuts.
The forest steadily devours the outer fields
        while what remains of the fence rusts and sags.
The boundaries remain locked within the courthouse
        and those with a memory of the reasons why
        joined the liar's bench of angels long ago.
The farmhouse itself has been leveled,
        scarcely a trace of life beyond
        the riot of ragweed and dock
        where once the kitchen garden thrived,
        these determined weeds telling their own story
        of what's to come.
Hard to imagine the extravagance of order
        when the simplicity of ruin
        is everywhere evident.
Easy to imagine how lonely the landscape becomes
        when even the dead have lost their voice.

SEEING IS BELIEVING

See the rolling acres of pink flowers,
        the gray clouds of birds, their hovering?
Begin believing you can.

The letters are piling up inside the door;
        whether as alphabets or stories, puzzles you.
Think of the Persian rug, its thick sea of reds.

There are vast reserves of character here,
        characters with character.
Some have been known to live longer than you.
You can smile and offer a cobalt blue vase
        etched with silver.
 You can strike a match.

The widow on the balcony gives names to the birds:
        Edgar, Merl, Olive, Bertha.
Her husband died when the factory burned down.
This was the same year the church
        sold discounted magic
        with little paper tags.

They made fender welts in that factory to prevent
        the ingress of water, dust and the like...
There was a quince tree in the side yard, hard yellow
        beacons related to apples, good for grafting.
Grandmother made honey from them;
        maybe with some of that cheap magic.

It was a house with bleached wooden shutters that never closed.

Somehow, the window, with its view of the meadow,
        has now disappeared,
        although a cloud of sun-lit crows
        reminds me where to look.

It was franked in blue ink from the War Office in the city.
Perhaps her English had improved, perhaps not.
They were tough then. Never let on.

Even now, dead, they bear their suffering well,
            can light this room with a single match.
And the flowers have arrived
            despite all obstacles.
It is not the privilege of writing your name
            so much as the privilege
            of knowing your memory persists,
            that these letters can still assemble,
                        dance, and disturb.
But you already know this, don't you,
            hovering there,
                        in that meadow, watching
                                    as the window opens?

LOCUST GROVE

In memoriam: Charles Burchfield

The blue-boned, stiff
    frenzy of winter
        amidst which
            a hill raises its long shoulder
                upon pools of light,
                    snow and sun,
                        shimmering.

WITHOUT ONE PLEA

The leaves of winter are flowering
        in the nervous wind of the new year,
        slender drifts of pale brown, ocher and umber:
            they murmur, but do not speak.
Among them my dog continues her long sleep
        under stones I gave her for a blanket
        on a warm day in June,
        a day removed from the calendar
        and kept near the heart.
Above her, a winding coil of ivy sheathes the ironwood green,
        and a few ragged clouds tumble from their blue roof,
        ready for a new destination,
        just as I am, just as I am.

IT'S FOOLISH TO GO LOOKING

It's foolish to go looking for the dream
      where you last set it down—that pillow
      of sweat and regrets no help on this road,
      this road meandering
      through small hills brimming with violets.
And those nocturnal screams under the drumming rain
      may probe your guts but carry no elucidation, no charity.
The diary written in your arthritic, illegible hand:
      is that blood, or bleat, or just blather?
Another day, more of the sky telling its stories,
      more of the earth listening to footfall and despair,
      and not one word to navigate the wild noise.
You are approaching the sea.
You turn your nose
      from the foul piquancy of fish, breathe
      a memory you'll carry to bed tonight
      in hope of oblivion and,
      should the old familiar dream find and surprise you,
      you can take comfort
      it found its way here
      almost as easily and quickly as you.

CAT BURGLAR

An old moon, pale as honeycomb, lifts
       over the jumble of roofs, the sharp tilt of the chimneys,
       and escapes for a moment the racing clouds.
Below, it is a good night for a thief, his step
       will go unnoticed under the scurrying wind.
It is one of the old professions,
       and he is good with his hands
       and knows things others don't, watches,
       observes the little habits of his neighbors,
       keeps a timetable, knows which doors are which,
       which windows they crack for air, knows
       that breeze, its restless sweeping of the brittle leaves,
       knows it is his friend if he can stay in sync
       with its whimsical pulse, remain
       patient and alert.
A poet might learn a thing or two,
       hair-strung over such silence,
       treading lightly upon the eggshell paths,
       following the tiptoe shadows down deserted alleyways,
       slipping past and through and out
       of doors and windows, casements and cellars,
       inhabiting a sixth sense, studying
       the arcane craftsmanship
       of blades and locks, hairclips and gloves, ball bearings
       and the carefully measured placement of a dollop of oil.
If he can but anticipate the ending,
       uncover the jewels, the cash,
       the hidden heart of it all,
       and then find with his cold eyes, that last step—
       dwell there, noiselessly, before his foot
       treads a fatal crease in the ancient floor—
       outfit himself this moment
       with a cloak finely woven as a poem,
       the theft and thief invisible under it,
       the perfect cloak within which to sail
       when all the sirens awake the night
       with the weary shock of their familiar song.

RUNNING THE CHANCES

Was it just the rattle of the old pick-up,
      the groaning squeal of brakes
      that made him think of her?
He was sitting on a park bench without a map
      stranded between two mountains.
The fortitude of stones and gravity lay upon him.
He was feeling almost lonely, a lost star,
      when a distant whistling of an old tune
      crawled into the last hour of light.

The distance between two points is some kind of number,
      cousin to truth, but there he was, autumn well advanced,
      and not only was there no toothbrush but
      his phone wouldn't work, so how could he know
      anything without its electric pulse?
He remembers her telling him there was more to
      everything than meets the eye
      and so the sky rose up to meet him,
      large words in crayon littered across the landscape.

And the children on those bicycles talked
      with hay straw in their voices and spider webs of
      memories from the long ago.

It was time to light candles in the big house
      and pour burgundy into
      the stiff hands of their smoky glasses.
It was time to untie the skiff and float into the umber sheen
      of an icy lake where words and numbers coalesced
      in a singularity adamant as graphene and viscous as sorghum.
It was time.

He would spend the night here, bend his circles
        within hers, defeat biometrics with sleek inter-lockings,
        kissings, and a sexual science unknown to their parents.

And when they came down the silken stairs to earth,
        the morning would have arrived, renewed
        within the green cradle of these venerable mountains,
        and he'd no longer be lonely, but whistling as if
        there were children somewhere who knew their names
        and if he'd run his chances, well, he'd have no complaint.

REUNION

On a bridge the old ones study
      how the night flows below them.
Willows sag in the still air.
Nameless shadows wade into water.

The newly released prisoner stumbles his blistered feet
      along a path, his legs brittle
      as his unfamiliar bones move again.
There's a house somewhere in the quiet
      whose beds are empty
      and where a chained dog circles, whimpering.

Reunions are a promise of impossible intentions, blue
      as autumn when the sun burns
      the corn with fevers no calendar anticipates.
Eyes like marbles, their bloated corpses are free now
      of disappointment and their son
      lost on an old road in a new world.

LUSH LIFE

for Jenny & Nathan Wilson

An ice-hot tune jazzes down the street,
      lush-life sax counterpointed
      by a piano picking its way
      like a fox through the hen house.
Fermentation. *Sturm und Drang.* Venerable.
A venerable dive filled with fermenting potheads, poets, and plebes.

Of God we had talked like doctors
      about to break bad news.

The door opens again and out spills
      a little dance with snare and brushed cymbals.

In less time than I can imagine
      all the news will be old news,
      and I'll hear mother again
      crying in the kitchen,
      and behind the bedroom door
      I'll be staring at the crucifix,
      its chipped paint revealing
      plastic, not revelation.
Still, the loneliness of that man
      on his cross is profound.
I learned to worship such loneliness slowly,
      and is, I suppose, why
      this bluesy jazz with its uneven, beating heart
      has me stopped now, under the lamplight,
      in a *distingué* attitude of prayer.

If I should call you, raise you from your sleep,
      will you understand how even your little resurrection
      in picking up that phone
      has me clicking my fingers, tapping
      my feet, wondering
      if there was something we missed,
      if the loneliness wasn't the mush of love
      finally burning itself out of our way?

THE PICNIC TABLE AT DUSK

The salt and pepper stand mute
        below two candles busy being beautiful.
You can see across the wide, serene plain
        of gold and scarlet tablecloth
        there's enough mystery to satisfy
        any number of theologians and poets.
There's enough, too, to repay the diligence of translators
        and the assiduity of hermetic lexicographers.
There's even enough to send me for a Manhattan
        on my way to my shrink and
        for my shrink to lay on the couch
        beside me, to weep, to confess, to say
        just look at those flames, just look
        at those stars, just look
                at your grandmother's salt and pepper shakers,
                how still they are, how reverent, fine, and perfect.

RED HEN AND SMALL WOMAN

A red hen goes scratching inside its small house
      while the hail gravels the roof
      and I watch a bent woman walk resolutely on
      into the racing fog and wonder where she's going.
Cows moan, horses nicker, the rooster crows once as if its neck's broken.
The famous quiet *before* descends, approaches complete stillness
      except for the slender trill of the random breeze.
Then the Oz scenes:
      the tin roof on the corncrib flaps and screams,
      dust wraiths flute into the black afternoon.
The farm sleeps on.
And in a corner of the canvas the sky begins to lift its blue eyelid.
Eventually, the storm rolls up its coven of loud children
      into its gray rug and goes off home.
Mother yells for us to come out of the storm cellar
      now the morbid fear of tornado's gone.
Grandfather smiles.
Myself, though, fixed at the window, hidden,
      am following that woman as she goes further
      on into something I think is longer and deeper
      and wider and more dreadful and wondrous
      than any of my mother's fearsome storms.
I crawl into Grandfather's lap.
When I begin telling him what I saw and what I think
      about who that small woman is and where she's gone
      and what might become of us all, he keeps smiling.
The sun shone, the crops showed solidarity and rose up, drought stayed away,
      as did locusts and frogs and other wild misfortunes.
The fog will come again.
The storm will rain with ice.
The chicken will scratch for kings and queens.
Then the small woman will come, doggedly walking,
      and grandfather go on smiling, holding still,
      as will we all, when the weather decides it's had enough,
      and we grow patient, at last, waiting and listening hard
      to the thin sound of that hen scratching
      for something a boy might plant
      that takes him to the stars.

TWO

"There are so many fragile things, after all. People break so easily, and so do dreams and hearts."

—Neil Gaiman,
Fragile Things: Short Fictions and Wonders

HALLOWEEN STORM

There's nothing glorious in dying. Anyone can do it. —John Lydon

The bones fly without effort tonight,
      their flesh flags rippling,
      their tarnished stone knuckles testifying
          that I may have run out of luck, my work
          become a toss of the dice.
Even so, they speak, and I listen
      to their choir of major and minor keys,
      femur and tibia, fibula, patella, tarsus
      and metacarpals, and all those delicate phalanges,
      listen to a choir breathing and speaking
      the song that stands between these many skies
      and all the leaden ghosts of belief.
What good are they anyway?
Hard, fragile, contradictory, countering
      the brain's obsession with continuation.
And all that blood and muscle, those nerves and nodes,
      and all the rest that makes no sense when it goes?
What use the phlegmatic carburetors within
      mixing life with a fine spray of temptations?
Take my hand.
The sweat is real, the danger more
      as we tightrope over the abyss of America:
          the mad coyotes with their yellow eyes are grinning.
Still, we have this cemetery for retreat.
Everyone *here* agrees that, though collagen once ruled,
      held things together, and does so no more,
      they're not sad, but happy for the chance to fly,
      to show us to the best seats for the black parade.
Do you hear them whispering?
We need go no further now
      than where we are
      to find the place
      beyond which dreams
      no longer campaign.

A MESSENGER COMES TO ELK RIDGE

after Jean Anouilh

The innocent get trapped, like in a cave, and a rope dangles,
    a knife slashes, the wicked stare at their darker mirror.
This boy from the far mountain carries a clear splinter from that mirror
    back to the home from where it came.

* * * * *

The path tonight through the beech wood
    is hard, frozen hard, hard to see, and long.
Only occasionally the moon springs loose a flash
    of luminescence from the frost-glistered snow.
The stars offer their thin light, and the breeze moves slowly,
    nearly silent, few leaves left to whisper secrets.
Such news he carried would need few words.
They were heavy words, stones from long ago
    with strange markings, abrasions of bone,
    just enough to read.
The cabin stood hiding just below the crest of the hill.
Moonrise had not yet found it, only a wisp
    of smoke shimmered as if carrying the last light of ghosts
    whose names he had never known.
Still, he knew now that it was their names he was carrying
    in the small satchel inside his heart.
There were three steps, a lariat of onions hanging forgotten
    on an overhead beam of the sagging porch.
Husbands with pride, brothers with drink, and rifles, sisters,
    daughters and mothers with loyalties,
    and so much blood to soak out of these ancient oak boards.
They wouldn't kill the messenger, but he'd never again
    be welcome on this ridge.
The fisted God, the only-one-chance God, had them in His grip now.
No, he'd be as unwelcome
    as the older gods who increasingly kept to themselves.
Cursing and tears echoed behind him.

He would walk to the river
      with his bundle of books and a single candle.
He knew how to cobble together a raft good enough
      to float him downstream and away, far away from here.

UNION ORGANIZER

A clearing dawn and the fever
       collapses as an angel walks the far hill,
       as a man chisels a few words free.
They begin searching his warm room.
Then, free citizens, they wander the property, looking
       here, and here.

He whispers at the bars of the window
       where the light climbs its blue ladder,
       where a child dances.

Heaven is a lonely place.
There are no thrones,
       only easy chairs, easy breaths,
       the flicker of a white moth.
The gears with which the old words turn
       are well-oiled testimonies.
They lean their shoulders into
       the silent work of hanging on.
And he does.

WELCOME HOME

There used to be a real me, but I had it surgically removed. —Peter Sellers

The sky tapped at the window
       he'd opened every day
       back when there was work
       and sleep and
       sometimes even love.

Late April and the world had tipped over into spring,
       birch keys hanging from clusters
       of pale, green leaves.
A soldier returned from war and his wife's bed too warm.
He opened the window, let out the old smell,
       wondered about all the new ones.

In the rain the white bones of the sycamore
       gleamed where lamplight fell
       out of the window and found them.
He'd climb that tree with his claws, find
       a path when the clouds parted
       and the moon burned each shadow
       into giving up their secrets.

The lilac smelled like perfume.
The dead groundhog smelled like home.
The rotting tubers were only garnish.

It was too early to tell if these broken images
       could give any more relief
       than feeling the gentle recoil
       of an M4 set against stone
       finding an anonymous target
       as faceless as her new lover.

WAITING FOR AN EXPLANATION

The gods of wisdom have all fled: Minerva and Apollo,
      Odin, Uncle Ira, Tom Terrific, Sherlock, Watson.
And the winter hills are ablaze with yellow flowers
      with no one to tell me what this means.
Words sweep through the house,
      cowering under tables, catching
      under the door sill, mumbling
      and pleading incoherently.
The shepherd down the lane,
      stubble on his cheeks,
      is still a boy with freckled arms
      shining red from sunburn
      from following, as he does each day,
      the lost ones without names.
There is a forest beyond the river impatient
      as an x-ray with its secret cancers,
      black bones, and stories
      of what's yet to come.
The sky comes over the hill
      lugging its bags of bruised ice
      while below the exquisite locusts,
      eager to chew their way
      through the last fields of hope,
      persist with their lamentations.
It all appears to be a day like any other
      to the man sitting quietly
      astride my fence, chin
      in the palm of his hand, blind
      with omniscience like all the other gods.

WILD ROSE

In Memoriam: Timothy Russell

The barges drift through the river's shadows
      untouched by the weight of the stars.
There are, as well, these amber ingots slowly molding themselves
      out of a different fire into the law we swear will hold.
Inside the mill tiny men work their brooms, clearing
      away tears from the continued manufacture
      of obsolescent dreams.
The Man of Sorrows looms over them from the altar.
The priest, with his back turned, is collecting
      his own share of the silence.
Before the villages spilled out from Pittsburgh,
      there were still those who remembered
      the Mingo's lament but now
      there's not one left to mourn
      the extinction of beast, forest, people.
Without science, but with smoke and imagination,
      there once stood a transparent wisdom
      under that elm at the edge of the clear cut,
      a mind could call down the stars
      and map any landscape with militant accuracy,
      a map could show the many houses of gods
      more familiar and powerful
      than the underfed skeletons of their replacements
      who have only words to move them
      from one flimsy pew to the next
      and no idea how time past becomes
      this beautiful wild rose
      rooted in what has always
      been headed our way.

TRAFFIC STOP WITH DUI

for Kevin Rippin & Val Nieman

I like that they're mostly blue sirens these days.
We were laughing so hard, of course, it didn't register
      until we'd gone blocks beyond your errant driving.
We rehearsed a fool-proof script for another few blocks
      then, with appropriated innocence, demure demeanor,
      you'd stopped and let down your window.
Did the policeman get to say anything?
I'm not sure, but do know you did get said
      what needed to be said:
        "Officer, it was the *panna cotta*,
        yes, that and no other, it was tipping over
        and I'm sure you understand we
        couldn't allow that, no sir, not ever,
        and, yes, then, I did swerve to right the
        said Italian confectionary, swerved right
        and left, multiple times, yes, that would be right."
"You folks haven't been drinking by any chance, have you?"
"No, Sir, absolutely not, Sir, only *panna-cotting-ing* it, Sir!"
Which I thought sounded extremely funny and which
      must've been because we did laugh as if it had truly been
      extremely, absolutely, and gut-wrenchingly funny!
I think now, though, that perhaps we overplayed our hand
      at that juncture for it was then he asked us all to
      please, step out of your car.
And we did, pleasantly, laughing, and trying to assume
      Hollywood compliance by lifting arms high
      which I don't think he actually asked us to do
      but which must have been impressive to see,
      our arms raised, straight up to morning, and still laughing.
Curiously, though, none of us could walk the proverbial
      straight line but we were laughing so hard
      how could we?
I'm sure alcohol had nothing to do with it.

Still, after we'd paid our fine, and someone's uncle's brother
        bailed us out in the wee hours, and we got back
        to your house, I did see the two empty fifths of Jim Beam
        on the table beside all the sympathy cards
        and remembered that your mother's bed was
        to be forever and ever eternally empty now
        and wondered then how it was no one had thought
        to say why it was we were drunk, half-crazy with grief
        and that the *panna cotta* was your mother's favorite
        and truly we did somehow want to make it right
        knowing somehow we never could.

SMALL TOWN HOSPITAL

Two white butterflies invade the pasture, alight
          on the bowed, wire fence below the blue ash.
The rust trembles under their weightlessness.
She's watching from the concrete pad where the hearse loads.
Tosses her gum, straightens her blouse, wonders
          about that taste, that taste in the mouth after blood.
The river tug's gray horn jars the quiet
          dance of this yard-sticked afternoon,
                    its light and shade.

The china clinks on the bone saucer.
A circle. A spill. Shaky hands.
He's only thirty-four.
This house a mansion that's seen its share of lovely teas.

Of all hours of the night long ago, she thinks.
Nursing was more muscular then.
He has hairy arms.
So she knows there will be shaving to come below.
Maybe more.
The dog circles the bed.
Whimpers, collapses.
Tail goes *thunk-thunk*.
Some things don't change:
          the carrot jello, Mass on Sundays, side-rail beds.
It would be good to slow down, watch the fields.
The redbud waves its branches, a desperate beckoning.

Esther Merinar, eighty-four, is sitting
          on the park bench below the verandah
          smoking her daily Winston.
The coal barge's surf wakes the green river.
All this happening between four and five in an afternoon?
Miracles. Desperation.
And which part, now, was the story she meant to tell?

The cabbages have fat, green worms.
She stops, stoops, picks them off,
       flings them onto the graveled path.

She's tiptoeing a tightrope in her white uniform.
She claps her hands over her ears gently.
Voices land delicately upon the silence
       between all these holes in her head,
           between what's here and what's gone ahead
               into the weeping flames of the afternoon
                  and will not surrender.
Another stick of gum,
     another enema,
        another bath,
           a hand job.
She's doing what's possible:
     the saint of herself
        anointing those she can
           with fingertips and unguents.

YOUR TERMS

We were told to wait,
and we did,
for awhile,
long enough for bees
to travel
across distances
hard to imagine
in the vaguely green
afternoon
beyond a window
somewhere
along the Hudson.
But you said you were tired
and didn't want
to spend another night
from home,
that the doctors
really were quite wrong,
or was it right?
I can't remember now,
because, you see,
while we were
thumbing old *Redbooks*
and *Geographics*
and those rogue cells
were doing their
multiplication hoochie-koo,
you were genuinely sick,
and tired
of hurrying up to wait;
you just wanted
something, anything
to happen,
hurried or otherwise,
but would wait

for it now to come
to you, your terms:
at home, your easy chair,
whatever was easiest . . .
And so we left,
when we should've
said something else,
tried once more,
heard out one more
possibility, but
we obeyed you, again,
and hurried,
not to wait any more,
but hurried home
to be ready,
and this different than
defenseless waiting,
different even than aggressive
hurrying.
You were exhausted, too,
let's be fair, but,
next morning,
from your walker,
you fried up
pancakes, read
the paper, watched
an old Masterpiece,
then finished
Mansfield Park,
aptly proving you were
right, and we were wrong,
and a week later,
more than ready,
done with waiting,
you didn't come down,

finally patient with us,
it would seem, and
even more finally,
done with waiting
for us, for it,
long past waiting
for whatever time
it takes, for you'd
closed your eyes
and opened your arms,
and it had all come— it, us, even
the morning with its flowers,
and its bees.

CATHERINE

All that long morning she walked, her purse leaden with stones. *Justice*. She had known the moon and the light it gave to dancing. She had drunk the sweetest wine, tasted the sharpest chocolates, lay with a man who could conjure a sleep as addictive as any perfumed opiate. Her shoes pinched her toes. It brought tears to her eyes to imagine their vile bloom. A squirrel ran along the wires above her. A dog barked in the alley behind the fire hall. She hoped the men were sleeping. Papers and credit cards and photographs and her checkbook—it didn't seem like much to offer for justice. She didn't even know how far the courthouse was. Maybe such a fortress was impossible. *Be my strong rock, a castle to keep me safe*. As if the bruise under her eye wasn't bad enough, there were telltale scratches along her arm. Clichés they were under the bright lights of sensible men. *Custody*. *Ownership*. These were other words. Could one really own children?

She had been beautiful and once had drawn infinity into the very lap of an afternoon, an afternoon where she had lain a table as perfect as linen and crystal, silver and red tulips could make it, had drawn its lulling surf of luxury into her very home and been treated as if she were actually from the same world as all the sensible men.

Children who loved her played in the grass and went to bed with stories and cocoa. What more could she say? In England the judge would still have worn a wig. She would have liked that. Or a mask. No, that was a different office, a different man, a different century. But it was an execution all the same. After today, she would begin her final dying, drowning within the deep waters of herself. It would take longer but the sentence was the same as it would have been then. *Justice*, the word that empties all others.

WATCHING

A warren of clean, shiny rooms,
      each with an intricate array of fine tools
      within which lurks occasional genius.
He has come to be healed.
He hears voices from far off strangers
      who suddenly arrive, seem to know him
      inside-out, intimately.
There is a radio somewhere suggesting the other world continues.
He remembers the long row of city buses he passed on the way here,
      diesel fumes irritating the green fringe of the churchyard,
      how pleasing it might have been to have gotten on, and gone,
      maybe to the ballpark, a double-header, eaten up some time.
He's here now, though, on his back,
      studying a ceiling as if it were a star chart
      where he might affix his own name.
Couriers with cheerful faces carry their verdicts
      back and forth, invincible, and young.
He's convinced the doll-house chapel
      doubles as a crematorium, smiles
      at how much sense that makes.
Then, suddenly, he's on deck, and the crowd goes silent
      as his thirsty pain accepts the pellucid flow
      of morphine and, later, the cytotoxins
      he's been promised will kill something.
He remembers thinking it sounded like a good idea.
He remembers thinking, good, about time, eating it, getting eaten by it.
He remembers to stay alert, watch for the signs, watch
      for that fast ball, a curve, or the change-up
      he always forgets until it's too late,
      and in slow motion now watches
      as it crosses the plate of his heart,
      as the umpire pounds the air with his fist,
      as the umpire, in time, pronounces,
            outside of time,
               out!

REGRESSION

The old VW beetle was the sink where all our old hippie dreams went to die. First, the battery, then the fuel injector, then an axle—holy shit, an axle? I cut my ponytail for money which told me I was desperate. And you, you dyed yours for vanity whose mirror told you your own problems. The weeds choked our once pristine field of weed. The dead-head embroidery peeled off our bell bottoms and one elephant in the room wore a suit and tie, the other draped a Spade purse off her elbow. And when we cried together at night, it was a bad moon rising across a murky future someone other than ourselves had conjured from bubble gum and a heroin whose new name we couldn't even pronounce.

CONTINUOUS CARE

Orange peonies encircle the porcelain cup
      tangled with green and gold leaf.
He had asked for Haydn, the opus thirty-three, the *largo e cantabile*.
He had asked for Darjeeling.
He pushes back from the table, stands, looks about
      for some instruction, someone who knows.
On the sideboard, the teapot, coiffed in a dingy, cream-
      and-umber cozy, is indifferent to the crisis.
He turns to the table, grasps
      a chairback to steady himself.
A trapdoor has sprung.
He feels it.
The escalation of bird song
      pouring through the bright window
      is about to let in the future, all of it, and soon.
The sound says that freedom exists.
He tries translating, but three jays and a sparrow
      refuse to become the calming *largo* he needs.
The table now opens its arms—there is to be an audience.
He's careful, holds his hands together, is firm with them.
The wind stirs in the piccolos—cherry blossoms—a flock
      of petals flutter and settle upon the table, a few
      in his hair, and one upon the back of his left hand.
Each is scored with a single letter.
He thinks. . . . maybe he can gather, arrange,
      decode them, have before him
      a tale, a message, some clue?
He remembers the solace of the Haydn, wants to use it,
      looks again at the letters, feels
      the fragility of their blossoms.
To whom do they belong?
The lamp's halo excludes a few, and some
      have now fallen, invisible, upon the white carpet.
What losses in the tiny fissures of time.

How many irreplaceable domestic dictionaries
　　　　go missing in a life, a single day?
And to what tunes were they once scored?
Is he to be settled with only this sinecure,
　　　　to tend the losses from ineffable mischief?
He sits down again, waits, wonders
　　　　if the tea's still warm.

MARINERS

Two men sit talking, one voice with a whistle
      and the other a cough
      that marks their progress through the old stories.
Their shadows
      pool on the weed-clutched sidewalk
      below a paint-blistered bench.
Their necks are tilted,
      as if the weight of memory
      unbalanced their skulls.
And, perhaps, does—more deaths
      now than lives, with only these stories
      to raise those long gone
      above the shifting horizon.
And when their eyes meet to confirm
      the veracity
      in these ongoing resurrections,
          the tales they tell
          keep them afloat
              in that rearing ocean
                  on this, their voyage out.

IMPATIENT

The wrens exchange their whistled notes
      as the sun slides along the silvered branch.
The coffee and the radio are in tune,
      bitter with old news:
            his wool sweater, blue veins sunk within,
            proof against the cold.
He counts the slow drip from the eave's icicles,
      measures the pulse of things,
      considers the long lane, the night
         slowly crawling its length,
         chasing the light through the fingers
         of the elms, the milk can
         thrust up through the drift,
            a forgotten soldier, the rusted lip
            of the lid like blood from a time when
            cows lived here and their needs marked
            the hours, and the calendar was as extraneous
            as an old man numbering his grudges,
               as if all the news were old and in the way
               of what should have come next.

THREE

If by your art, my dearest father, you have
Put the wild waters in this roar, allay them.

—Act 1, Scene 2, *The Tempest*, William Shakespeare

IN BETWEEN

The gate is open
       between the golden trees,
       between the gray-bright stones of the cemetery
          where the squirrels run.
The caretaker knows where the bones bloom in the spring.
He covers them with the blood of baited trespassers.
The magic can't belong to just anyone,
       but comes when it's needed.
He lives alone in that little hut beside the muddy stream.
The window ledge is crusted with frost.
He has a name his mother knew.
In between the branches, the sky drifts
       toward the moonlight, its gift
       letting you see where to run.
Follow the squirrels.
See where their ghost tails flash.
He has a knife where his tongue was.
His gloves are only decoration.
The horror films were rehearsals
       with flashlights and your hand puppets.
Genre has nothing to do with it.
Today's casting calls for a flood, some bad dope, and a blue-haired librarian.
The children will be featured only after you turn your back away.
Count the seconds.
That's right.
It was only five beats.
He'll be playing solitaire again tonight.
Innocence.
He's having none of it but, if that's where you have to go, well. . . .
       in between the night and the dawn,
       that glimmering, that thin wavering wrinkle of light,
       there may be just enough of what you need.

OUT AND KNOWN

He hurries along the frost-brittle ledges of stone,
      hears the last bird in the last light.
Something in the tone
      of her voice puts him on edge,
           like the high wire, the tempting cliff
                for the suicide, the fool in love.

We all want to make sure the *what if*
      is found to be as true
           as we knew it to be
                when we believed truth was
                  and could be found
                      out and known.

Known . . . like this gurgling, rushing tumble
      of song from the hedge sparrows
           repeating and repeating and
                which, we know, for the night soon comes,
    but we hesitate, and that man
           races on ahead, fears fidelity like we do,
                falls to his death, and did he know
                  before it was too late
                    what he had to do?

We, too, hesitate, and suddenly
      the lamps come on, the night is here
           and we slip inside and drink
                dark porter and will ourselves to remember
                  the dunnock's song burst and remember, as well,
    Cuchulain driving clouds from our narrow skies,
           never doubting, no hesitation, happy to be
                whipping his sure death ahead of him
                  as if death cared no more for him than he did for it.

KNOWLEDGE

for John Freeman

What I know is only some days better
      than another's and so I set
      grandmother's little willow box carefully
      on an upper shelf and wait.
Patience, too, can be known as an experience
      within time, and no less valuable
      for how it measures out certain
      minutes, as if they could be known, too,
      and are, or have been, at least, on some days,
      known with what I might almost call certitude.
This is important.
I may need another box or, perhaps, simply,
      this coffee can with its green lid
      waiting patiently beside the enameled stove.

THESE DAYS

He'd had enough of the lawyers, the indemnity chits,
      the report cards, the arrogant fragments
      of morality and taste
      billboard-plastered across the landscape.
He would take the last exit, get a cool drink, sit at a window
      with a dumpster for a view, watch
      the tough sparrows take
      apart, with admirable diligence,
      their part of America.
He'd put in a quarter, a dollar, a fingernail, listen
      to an electric fiddle and accordion, something Parisian
      in this last roadhouse in West Virginia.
He'd go without romance, embrace Catullus
      until the words in *flagrante delicto*, or *in extremis*
      cried out "enough!"
The bright cars can go their own ways home, to their own scars,
      he'll let the burdock stand pretty
      in the vase at his table
      while outside that vain flag fades
      in the heavy light of history.
His bones will watch until they've had enough, then crawl
      off to this corner or that one, curl up, and pray
      the harsh lullabies of innocence.

NEELY'S RIDGE

Furious branches of sky
      rake shadows across the mountain.
The time has come to set sail,
      to launch these tea cups upon the open fields.
Here the tomatoes die discreetly
      with their papery leaves and bloody mush,
          and the drought persists without
              megaphones or politicians
                 and another century slinks out the door.
Soon the juries will all return
      and "best of show" again go unrewarded.
See, there where the dusk goes,
      that green flash of endless horizon,
          see there was something after all
              which was worth the telling
                 and this blood on your hands
                    will be mortal enough for both of us.

THIS FAR, AND . . .

The last good man draws a line:
    this far, and no further.
Justice will be served if he can just stay put,
    remain vigilant, remain. . . . something.
Sleep comes no more.
A purple shimmer of sunlight wrinkles
    the horizon beyond which
    the ocean falls into night.
He is as disturbed as good men often are,
    weeping and moaning.
It is not like Job in Indiana after
    the basketball team loses.
It is seeing his favorite dog
    skinned alive by teenagers
    bored, high
    in twenty-first-century America.
It is the pink slip after twenty years
    of saluting the flag, saying yes-sir, of turning the cheek.
It is the Dear John letter in the pink envelope
    returning a ring, a flower, his own good words.
He draws the line with a deluxe Parker pen.
Imagines Charles Atlas drawing a line in the sand
    and winning all the fair-haired lasses
    back when the world beat the bullies.
Still, he must retreat.
He picks his battles, re-draws the line.
And keeps re-drawing the line, again, and again,
    moving it back a little further
    each day, surrendering, eventually,
    more than he ever thought could be surrendered.
The line has become a circle now
    within which he can just fit, naked,
    and from which he lifts aloft
    a small, white flag.

It is ignored—pathetic.
He screams the word, *pathetic*, and again, and finally
        hisses, one more time with spit and venom: *pathetic!*
The feeling he gets then
        is almost like when
        he first drew that first line.
Almost.
It makes him wonder what he thought it meant
        to take a stand.
He smashes his fist on his mother's table,
        orders his sample of Viagra,
        and wanders back to the beach,
        confident, and no more a man
        than any junkie
        with a smile
        and a needle
        he swears
        points true north.

A DOZEN FOR EMILY

In memoriam: Emily Carr

Finally, the wild trees
dance
and the divine chaos
returns,
our only partner.

ELMER

I could see the bent man bend, climb down
        out of his mud-washed Chevy pick-up
        and limp towards the porch.
After eighty hard years on the farm
        he still kept pace with kindness.
He seemed to appear from behind the sofa
        where I lay breathless
        and quiet, waiting on my fever
        to crumble and reassemble
        as buttered toast with blackberry jam and tea.
It happened that way on good days
        when I wasn't dying, though I expected to
        any day in those scarlet-fevered, month-long days.
He'd brought me a toy trumpet
        and a corny joke about a smart-alecky mule,
        as well as a comic book, *The Green Lantern*,
        and a piece of cake from Aunt Hettie.
Later that cold spring, he lifted me
        onto his lap behind the huge wheel
        of the Farmall tractor and we lumbered
        across the ink-black soil
        destined to become tobacco, corn, and hay.
The wind was fresh and my lungs filled
        with simple and miraculous air
        and I shivered now,
        without fever, and believed
        the field would soon be dotted
        green with crops and hope.
I believed then, too, that I would live
        to tell a story almost like this one.

LINES

A dozen perfect lines
     draw the color
     into this painting
     they'd been dreaming
     as if they were strangers.

A Merlin draws a line
     directly across the high clouds,
     then stumbles, brakes,
     and falls away
     back into the trees,
     unlucky warbler
     headed south no more.

You begin to pay attention, lake gravel
     at your feet, and try to place a word
     on your tongue where the first rain drop
     could land and, if simultaneously,
     just the kind of miracle
     that connects all the dots.

There is a house on a hill,
     chimney smoke, a dog's bark,
     and a door opening outwards
     like a hand shake.
You will think the path
     is a straight one
     and try going there today.
You walk miles and get no closer,
     draw the forest's single shadow
     close about you.

Tomorrow, you cast a limp line
        onto the black lake and wait
        for the silver leap
        of a striped bass.
You had planned this much
        as the night's dream unraveled
        and spoke.

You are unkempt from a night in the woods,
        apologize, ask directions of a stranger,
        and together you study these lines
        on the palm of your hand,
        lines like a map or work of art,
        and then he points across the meadow
        and tells you the door's open
        and you should make yourself at home.

There's fish for supper that night.
Later, the stranger discusses the painting
        on the wall, a painting you say
        reminds you of home,
        the lines there leading you
        back through time into
        this almost familiar present.

THE OTHERS

To the south, where the Pennsylvania Railroad crosses the creek over a simple stone arch, I see the smallest flicker of movement, a slender blue filament of color, vertical, unnatural, quivering...but as its long neck turns to me and then subtly away I've seen that I'm seen: a great heron still in the still shadows of the still stream, seeing, and waiting. Winter is well established, late December, and the far south far away. There is a story but it isn't mine, nor is it finished yet. Were I closer to the earth, native to it, I'd guess there's a sacrifice in progress, and with it some thing will take a greater hold on life. Someone's mouth full of blood and feathers will carry one thread. Perhaps a crow or a turkey buzzard and, if the latter, will be flossing its horny beak afterwards. And as the sun, the wind, the frost, and the slow absorptive veins of the soil advance and add their warp and woof, they begin not to finish but complete. And me, I'll hold up this thread once light, now words, perhaps still aquiver and, if lucky, transparent with the ways of the nameless gods who've not yet left us here alone in this lonely land.

APPARITION

There were these plums, their six shadows,
       unevenly hanging in the breeze-tousled branches.
Other black boughs held sparks of light, bright ghosts
       among the trembling foliage.
And all was quiet except for the distant rumbling
       rattle of a train on the abandoned tracks
       running through the neighbor's valley.

STATIONS: BEECH GLEN

Ablaze. A puddle of wind-fallen apples littered upon the lawn waiting. . . .

They have waited despite the other great events of the day.
They have waited under a gray sky speeding to rejoin the squadrons of rainbows
    and moonbeams and crows and bats and clouds and kites and planes with bombs.
They have waited and I grow sentimental about them, want to hold them to my breast
    and cry over them, my tears filling their worm-shriven bruises with crystal and
    permanence and a patience as pure as theirs.

Nothing lasts but this.

The tears are worth everything you put into them.

They are worth nothing.

And a fountain not made by hands is worth everything.

There was another tree in the garden, too. Apple?

If it makes you feel better, call it a pomegranate.

Some things are made to last. Like that story.

I will take these apples to Roy McCardle, a man who still knows what to do with things
    . . . .like apples, how to pluck the Jonathans and Spies from the basket
    crawling with yellow jackets and get stung
    not nary once since'n I was a boy
    and tumble them into the hopper and crank
    the mead of the Americas
    into the same tin cup he used to feed me spring water
    trickling over a moss-edged sandstone ledge deep in the hills.

I'm still here.
I keep coming back for more.

Though west of Eden,
I feel the east wind blowing up the hollow
and Roy's ghost touching me on the shoulder
as he shows me the way home
past the frack-poisoned pasture.

Cry over our world and watch it fade outside the window into autumn, red chrysanthemums and purple asters with fat warblers whistling in high elms, and the sky slowing down to watch over us letting the sun through long enough each day for the miracle.

And the sun shone and the rain fell and
the land grew with stories about the day
before that one and the one before this one
and this following the ever after
when you were born inside a blood-riven womb of tears.

Apples. Cider. Northern Spies. Harshmans. Scouts in Bavaria in the Middle Ages. Tears. Apples. First of
October, yellow jackets a trembling skin on the old press where Roy turns the crank, squeezing out the lemony-gold juice, the sky running down the hill into the early evening haze lifting from the hollow.

Windfalls.
Seasons slipping away into another.
Death eaten up by life.
He never got stung.
He's gone now. However,
    it did take ninety-three years to catch him.

Not bad. I can't complain.

Windfall: sudden and unexpected piece of good fortune. . . .

A FEW OF THE BIGGER NOTIONS

If that fiddle can ever fish me out of this heavy room
      and onto the lawn with its green arms open
      wide to the dancing trees. . .
well, then, let me find once more those words
      of light, the divinity wafers that melt
      on the tongue, that sugar the songs
      each should sing
and make me, as well, the unwitting but pliant
      oracle of serendipity and serenity,
      of sweet paradox and
      the better accidents of providence so that
when our arms find each other tripping the light fantastic,
      embracing every dance with fervor
      and hilarity, let that moment after
      be the kiss where oblivion reigns
      with its promise of eternity.

A MAN

Wet sunlight on a brick church where
        under the upturned bowl of the nave
        flame candles and prayer
        as overhead a hospital helicopter
        carries its own secret urgencies.
Beyond the city the fields remain asleep,
        the fencerows alone singing
        in the freshening breeze.
The coffee steams in its white cup, patiently
        cooling as a man walks back and forth
        with decisions yet unmade.
Such times as these call for portents and poetry,
        but the familiar will again arrive
        without consulting us:
                someone dies
                wanting
                someone near.
The coffee grows cold, the prayers go
        unanswered but the fields are important,
        their old earth hungry
        with an urgent longing to be worked
        even as the songs slip unnoticed
        through the singing wires.
Far away the gathered prayers lift their lonely petitions
        even as the acolyte without a concern in the world
        snuffs each candle and drags his way
        back through the sacristy into a world
        hurrying to dinner, a world
        where fields matter little and decisions
        get made with easy and careless confidence.

WHAT IF WE KEEP TRYING

*To all the little children: the happy ones; and sad ones;
the sober and the silent ones; . . . [and] yes, the good ones, too;
and all the lovely bad ones.* —James Whitcomb Riley

Today there were children at the door.
I gave them erasers shaped like fingers
   and wondered later if they knew about pencils.
The birds sang their names in the high branches
   of the yellow sky with its blue sun.
You were deaf, but loved to lean your head
   as if it was natural to keep trying.
With all these doctors, you would think things
   would work out.
I remember stitches in my gut woven with piano wire.
Not a single note was struck I'd ever heard before.
Agony found fear its partner
   in the polypropylene's slow adjustment to flesh.
What if they fall on the steps and bleed, those children,
   and I can't hear their screaming song?
And all the doctors are gone without numbers or names?
And you, you keep leaning toward something, you keep trying.
I look up to see the sky changing, and worry
   about what I can say if one of them returns
   to the door, tears streaming down
   her face, blood on her hands and knees.
And who's to pass judgment if there's nothing to be done
   but hope the birds sing once more?
This time, I promise, I'll remember the words
   to the one song that might lead us safely home
   where doctors pay house calls and offer
   lollipops to children, even the bad ones.

CRAYONS

Amid the litter of
       greens and blues, oranges and yellows,
       two girls point and yell,
       demonstrating with voices and bodies
       the purpose of pigment,
       paper, breath, and their breath
       let loose, their words out flung
       creating a speech pulled
       from little lungs and brains brimful with news.
Their mouths stretch, and with their eyes
       they illumine this rebirth of language,
       shaping it for you to speak, as well,
       inside this endless room
       in which they've conquered time.

That only one child is yours, no matter;
       the other runs, too, as lovingly—
       arms open, a kiss, believing
       in your goodness by the other's example,
       an example telling you the responsibility
       is never simple to live for another day
       when such innocence might come to you,
       to sit with you, to speak to you,
       that language of theirs before ours
       lost now to paradise.

Some will tell you to enter their embrace
       and discover what living can hold—
       enough, this feeling here that love had
       before it was reduced by repetition and sex.
Some will tell you it's unlucky to remember anything
       beyond these moments . . .
       and then they go missing somewhere beyond you.

Some will tell you to follow love into the nursery
        and break all the clocks there
        and return, renaming the world
        with words so enflamed with prurient goodness
        they sear a delicate maze where
        meaning navigates its way within the skull:
        so many good intentions, so little to do.

You will see
        their ceaseless creating, their chattering mouths,
        their somersaulting intelligence, their tongues and lips joined
        to whistle, to sing their hand-clapping dances.
You will see all this, these little creatures
        displacing nothing with such infinitude
        that you'll feel something slow within yourself,
        memory sluggish from its daily dredging of words,
        slowing until finally you arrive here beside me
        dumb, listening, listening to these children tell the wonders
        which have carried their lives
        toward a place we have called the future.
They call it home.

THE WINTER BOX

Somewhere beyond the edge of the planet
    the sun crawled away
    and the motionless cold
    built its winter box around me.
Still, over that southern hill
    a thin brush of cloud
    scrapes away enough gray
    to leave a blush of peach.
Earlier, I followed a dog named Max
    on a circuitous trail of his own choosing.
I had many questions but he was impatient
    and had little time for me,
    his black eyes inscrutable.
I'd thrown tea leaves
    from breakfast onto a snow bank.
Could I have read them, intuited ideograms from the divine?
It was Christmas time,
    but I'd found no angels
    except the sad one above me
    teetering lop-sided from the crown of the tree,
    a tree headed to the land-fill day after tomorrow
    and after that a new year.
I'll sing the saddest songs I can find—
    Christmas in Prison, Hello in There—
    and do as I always do,
    throw words
    ahead of me and follow,
    hoping against hope,
    as Father liked to say,
    which now I hear
    sounds pretty hopeless.

TRANSLATION

Mythology is to relate found truth to the living of a life.
—Joseph Campbell, *The Hero's Journey: Joseph Campbell on His Life & Work*

Twin dormers atop a white Cape Cod
      and pre-Technicolor green forest
      rolling away up steep, sunny hills.
That was just one corner of what he'd come to see.
Another, a coffee shop with hipsters, stale scones,
      and a teen-age barista impersonating her grandma.
And the third, a vacant lot, for sale, weeds, a forgotten vote-for-me
      politico's sign rotting as swiftly as the politician.
The last? A cemetery between highway
      and suburbs haunted
      by squirrels, snakes,
      and a marauding troupe of domestic deer.
Still, there were names here he'd thought
      to have forgotten who raised up
      their marble letters, spoke and,
      as they spoke, assembled faces
      capable of scaring the bejesus out of him.
A deep breath, he tells himself, *a deep breath*.
And a deep breath was all it took to listen,
      and he did—they had a lot to say.
When later he passed below that house again,
      he felt as if those dormers were watching,
      felt as if they'd been listening, too,
      that there was something to be shared
      if only he could manage the translation.

ONE VERSION

I had to climb a mountain. There were all kinds of obstacles in the way. I had now to jump over a ditch, now to get over a hedge, and finally to stand still because I had lost my breath.
—Joseph Campbell, *The Hero with a Thousand Faces*

Down the glass mountain
      princes and eagles slide
      into histories
      no one reads
      while the star tree
      turns its face
      each day up
      and each night down
      to its feet
      where
      in a pool
      of milk-light
      comes the moon.

And inside
      that mountain
      is another pool
      into which
      a girl tries
      reading
      the future
      each night
      before laying
      her head
      on the pillow
      of rocks
      given reluctantly
      by a tribe
      of reduced giants.

During the day
          she paces
          the floor of
          her translucent cave
          and waits for a boy
          who's probably
          still asleep
          in a hay mow
          to finally wake
          and read the folktale
          will lead him
          on the breadcrumb
          trail of words
          to rescue her,
          guarantee love
          and youth
          and turn
          stars into apples
          and her icy room
          into hearth
          and home.

SYMBOLIC

The first function of mythology is showing everything as a metaphor to transcendence.
—Joseph Campbell, *The Hero's Journey: Joseph Campbell on His Life & Work*

Of course, the symbols were never going to work out the way you'd hoped. Too much confusion of one thing with the other leaving reality standing naked inside the rain, cold and real, just as your skin is proving to be despite the Italian shoes, the Brooks Brothers' slacks, your Burberry jacket. They'd seemed, and I agree, to be very real symbols—you would've thought they'd be enough.

Should you have, instead, worn a gold cross, genuflected, and bowed— tried out *those* symbols—would they have enabled you to avert. . . well, but what was it it was to be averted? The hero's descent into hell, that big sinkhole glowing with so much meaning right next door? Best not go there—no, not the hole! The Icelanders jump into burning holes all the time. No, avert the myth and folk tale, all that hero stuff, stories built out of symbols are suspect, all those unicorn horns, the apple seeds, the beanstalks and an inordinate number of misdirection cues concerning the road not taken, and whose mother is he in bed with anyway? No, avoid such tales, those strings and sinews of symbols only lead to deeper rabbit holes and remember how that worked out!

You know we never do see in all those ubiquitous velvet paintings Jesus naked with John at the Jordan but if, in fact, He really was naked, or *nekkid* as the Baptists say, well, then that story might just hold a little more traction than it currently does.

So, there you have it. Come in from that un-symbolic rain. Even with an umbrella, it's most inclement weather. I sure as hell am going back inside through the real door beyond which there's a real fire. And, as I say, you should as well, or at the very least, strip off all those expensive clothes, those useless symbols and get wet honestly—you'll either get pneumonia or get reborn real quick into that other world where the real story of your one real life might, yes, end, but it might just also truly begin. Call it resurrection, if you will, but let it go at that. No symbols, please.

NOT ALL THAT MUCH

for Doug Van Gundy

It wasn't all that much, you might say, nothing
      to write home about, just
      a heavy green floor of ground cedar and springy peat
      littered with reindeer moss and lichened stones,
      here and there evidence of flying squirrels,
      muddy punctures in the cloth of the moss,
      and coyotes, their ropey, black scat,
      and overhead a canopy of
      birch, beech, and red spruce,
      the latter the local's *yew pine* whose pointed, black lances
      bristle along the ridgeline.
Not that much, perhaps, and our only companion,
      a still and remembered, peculiar silence,
      a silence with weight,
      and the kind of karma you can't get
      from books, or gurus, or poets.
I lean against the gray birch,
      or sit on the white sandstone,
      or kneel in the faded leaf litter, and pray
      without thinking God or prayer,
      pray by simply staying put, letting
      time fall away from me, letting
      thought fall away from me
      until it's just me, and this, these
      things that don't seem all that much
      but are.

MATHEMATICS

Were the bane of my young life.
One plus one?
Well, o.k.
Adding and subtracting, too.
Two plus two?
Sure, innocent enough.
Multiplying, dividing?
Well, again, o.k., I guess,
        but in small doses, please.
And the rest?
Fractions, decimals, quadratics, calculus?
You cost me scholarships and
        more stress than I ever thought possible.
And story problems?
Story problems!
From second grade until forever,
        they made me catatonic,
                narcoleptic, dyspeptic.

And now?

Now I see how they built the pyramids
        and some day will take us to Mars.
Now I see how the bridges I cross every day
        depend upon their invisible assemblages.
Now I see them lurking in the DNA that lurked in the semen and ovum
        of the impossible equation of my parents' love-making.
Now I see that even the un-seeable Beyond
        might be seen with their precise maneuverings.
Even what lies beyond that Beyond, beyond the ineffable;
        that, too, might some day be found with these
        one plus ones, these two plus twos.
Seraphic Fibonacci. Pythagorean Monad.

Or just how the Tao begets One,
       and One begets Two,
       and Two begets Three,
       and Three begets all things.
Funny how they almost begin to sing
       as they close in on infinity.

URBAN RENEWAL

There was once a neighborhood
        below this roaring overpass.
The man holds his fedora up in one hand
        to shield his face as he looks
        beneath the last flash of sun,
        as if to sort through a personal newsreel
        of memories with which
        the past might be rebuilt.

I can see now the glimmering of twilight
        that must've chased the steps
        that led him to find his way here.
Despite the traffic, crickets can be heard
        ticking their involute and steady notes—
        a kind of magic, perhaps, that will open
        the door for which he was looking.

He's putting on his hat now and bowing
        towards a cat picking its way
        across the field of bricks.
I can't hear the names they call each other
        but know they will have held close
        memories much like my own,
        each with places named and recalled
        as precisely as a doctor with his knife.

DOG DAYS

The shrill ringing of the locusts
      only helps bring lower that heavy sky.
The sun is seeping even into the shadows.
And the creek is shallow, and the snakes edgy, and the lizards
      quick and magical.
Believe me, in these hollows the heat can boil men's nerves to murder.
The thunder clouds lift their intricate crowns to the thin ceiling
      of an afternoon progressing in slow-motion.
Everyone has taken to whispering.
Alma whisper-chants nursery rhymes: *one-two, buckle my shoe. . .*
      three-four, get indoors. . . —find a fan, a friend, a story
      to tell the minutes down, how Jack brings snow from the crystal mountain.
And Pretty Polly will come, too, and drown again as the crickets start.
Who tells these tales matters little, nor that they are told true,
      just tell them well and cool will be
      the breaths taken in the long hours before bed.
And murder will again lust itself out along
      the banks of the Ohio or the Troublesome
      and just maybe a night breeze can be conjured
      before the stories run out altogether.
Later, hold your flashlight steady
      and thread your path with these stories,
      good enough compass for any home you choose.

Hindman Settlement School, 2010

POET IN THE SCHOOLS

A morning with cold in its teeth, wind turning the children
      in circles as they waddle from bus to door.
Amid the clamorous echoing of bells and lockers
        and the shrill bleat of the intercom reciting
        schedules, scores, bland menus
        of pizza-burgers, chicken fingers, and meat loaf,
        amidst all this these children survive.

In a brick box of a school I read
        them poems about Santa Claus and ice cream,
        the Creggan white hare, and all the ones with silly rhymes.
They squirm and fidget, bums flat on the hardwood,
        and smile, braces gleaming.
Some of them smell, others tell,
        without a word, about their home lives:
        his grunge tee, her stained skirt, another's nervous-lick eczema.
I mourn for them.

In the back the troubled ones sit strapped in wheel chairs
        with their lolling heads rocking, faces frozen,
        some more ragged, some more immaculate,
        each wearing their differences differently,
        tongues restless, eyes fixed and deep as any far universe
        with moans from little nightmares the rest of us
        only glimpse across a chasm of luck and privilege.

And after silently cursing a small prayer against genetics
        and certain of the happier gods, I breathe, go on, and surrender to what these
        poems are capable of, let the shrieking wail
        of goblins enter this cold gym, thrill them with the little orphan,
        let Seuss rhyme laughter with my banter, entice them,
        and swear to let nothing deny their deliverance from pablum into art, however
        defined— papier-mâché, songs, tales, poems, dance, drums.

I can not fail them: no amount of belching, farting and whispering,
      no joker sailing a wad of paper or meddling teacher over-reacting,
      no rumbling furnaces or groaning refrigerators will stop these words,
      nothing is to deflect them.
So, I tell the one about the family who lived on a mountain
      so high they had to keep rocks in their pockets to keep from being blown away,
      and then the one about how the songs we sing will one day save us. I tell them
      about heroes diving for the drowned, rescuing us with stories.

And now the room has grown silent,
      and I'm pleased, sure enough, and grateful, but then. . .
Then there's this smack, and a different silence, an embarrassed one,
      and another smack, then a kind of out of sync, awkward slip-slap,
      and I see embarrassment coming over the faces nearest—
      and the slapping becomes louder
      approaching assuredly some rhythm.
It's the boy in the wheelchair—
      cream turtleneck with a necklace of paper pumpkins—
      and he's straight forward, head up, his eyes finding mine
      and I return the gaze, maybe we all do,
      and into his deep universe fall,
      transformed,
      and his rhythm solidifies into what we all recognize now:
      he is . . . simply . . . clapping!

And now we are all
      clapping, together, all of us
      together as we should be,
      and I join this extemporaneous applause—
      knowing it's not for me at all,
      but for what he's found
      for every single one of us
      who's ever *not* been called on,
      who's felt hung out to dry, been picked last,

been poked, tripped, and toppled,
lost, strung out, yearning, abused, dying
somewhere out of sight
in our private universes, and he,
he has opened the rooms
of paradise
for us to see
how simply easy it is
to smile, as he is smiling, to smile,
and smile . . . and smile.

JUST HERE, WHERE THESE HORSES . . .

There is nothing left for me
but to live fully and completely in the present. . . —Thomas Merton

Not in a car,
> but on foot, through the knee-high field of bracken,
> upward, toward the cloud-torn rocks,
> the larks and sheep blending their music.

Not at a desk,
> but in a chair below the patulous shadows
> of the old ash anchoring the summer yard
> where a breeze arrives, in time, miraculously.

Not in a chair,
> but on your back, on a blanket on the ground,
> your hands behind your head, your face
> uplifted towards the topiary clouds
> where again you might roam the corridors of childhood.

Not in bed,
> but up early, before the sun, with a certain serenity
> to greet you, and you passing it along to partner, sweetheart,
> child, and taking them
> fishing or walking, swimming or dancing,
> as if your life depended upon it.

Not on the phone,
> but with pen and paper, key-strike and screen, patiently
> re-discovering yourself and dressing your affections
> with the respect that comes word by word,
> one after the other, patiently and intensely like Frost
> mending a wall.

Not at the queue in the bank,
          but in the forest look for
          a currency to redeem
          beyond tomorrow, look for
          a quiet to heal the times you forgot to say thanks,
          for the small change whose smile
          transforms the day outwards.

Not in school, not at work, not following orders,
          not clicking the mouse and chasing after,
          not fueling the economy, not in heat,
          not in charge, not *ever* groveling,
          not in a box, not in a binary system,
          but here, where these horses are.
Just here, an open, August field, unadorned and
          empty save for them, the air raw and alive,
          their bushy tails of straw, their thick necks,
          their muscular cords of sinew,
          the liquid pools of their dignified eyes . . .
                    with them, to be in their company,
                    a step can be taken, a breath
                    drunk that might be the saving of your life
                              and, if begun in time, the saving
                              of the world, as well, might begin
                              just so, just here, just now.

—*Brechfa Common, Powys, Wales*

ACKNOWLEDGMENTS

"August Ghosts," *Pine Mountain Sand and Gravel*, 2014

"Regression," *Pine Mountain Sand and Gravel*, 2019

"Neely's Ridge," *Anthology of Appalachian Writers*, 2012

"Stations: Beech Glen," *Anthology of Appalachian Writers*, 2014

"Halloween Storm," *Anthology of Appalachian Writers*, 2016

"Lines," "This Far and. . .," *Anthology of Appalachian Writers*, 2018

"Traffic Stop with DUI," "Following the Silence" [originally titled "Finding the Words For. . ."], *Anthology of Appalachian Writers*, 2019

"One Version," "Symbolic," "Translation," *Anthology of Appalachian Writers*, 2022

"In Between," *Yellow Chair Review*

"Running the Chances," "Out & Known," *Poetry Salzburg Review*

"Small Town Hospital" *Still: The Journal*

"Crayons," *Crosswinds Poetry Journal*

"Mariners," *Scintilla* [Wales]

"Poet in the Schools," *Paterson Literary Review* [2019 Allen Ginsberg Prize, co-winner]

"The Winter Box," "Impatient," *Kestrel*

"On the Edge of Time," Honorable Mention, Robinson Jeffers, Tor House Prize, 2019

"Elmer," *Appalachian Journal*

"Welcome Home," *The Bluestone Review*

"Red Hen and Small Woman," *Cutleaf*

"Without One Plea," *Pikeville Review*

"Not All That Much," *Appalachian Review*

"Knowledge" has been printed as a limited-edition broadside by The Costmary Press, Kent, OH, 2019

I cannot thank enough Doug Van Gundy and Anna Egan Smucker for their friendship and close readings of some of these poems, and as always my unbounded gratitude to Cheryl for more than I can say. Thanks, as well, to Kevin Watson for being so understanding and supportive.

NOTES

"Lush Life"

The title here refers to the jazz standard written by Billy Strayhorn from 1933 to 1936. It was performed publicly for the first time by Strayhorn and vocalist Kay Davis with the Duke Ellington Orchestra at Carnegie Hall on November 13, 1948.

"Not All That Much" is included in the volume *Dark Hills of Home*, Monongahela Books, Morgantown, WV, 2022

The fifteenth line in the poem "Continuous Care," is from the poem, "Allegro," by Tomas Tranströmer, as translated by Robert Bly

The epigraph for the poem "What If We Keep Trying" is the original epigraph for the poem, "Little Orphant Annie," by James Whitcomb Riley [1885].

"Despite the Hour" – Italicized lines drawn from Adam Zagajewski's "Farewell to Zbigniew Herbert."

Marc Harshman's *Woman in Red Anorak* (Lynx House Press) won the Blue Lynx Prize, and his poetry collection, *Believe What You Can,* was published by the Vandalia Press [West Virginia University] and won the Weatherford Award from the Appalachian Studies Association and was also named Appalachian Book of the Year by the Mountain Heritage Literary Festival in Tennessee. His fourteenth children's book, *Fallingwater: The Building of Frank Lloyd Wright's Masterpiece* (co-author, Anna Egan Smucker) was published by Roaring Brook / Macmillan. He is co-winner of the 2019 Allen Ginsberg Poetry Award, and his poem "Dispatch from the Mountain State" was printed in the 2020 Thanksgiving edition of *The New York Times.* His most recent publication was *Dark Hills of Home,* published by Monongahela Books in 2022 to celebrate his tenth anniversary as Poet Laureate of West Virginia. Marc has recently been commissioned to write a poem to celebrate the 40th anniversary of NPR's *Mountain Stage.*

www.ingramcontent.com/pod-product-compliance
Lightning Source LLC
Chambersburg PA
CBHW021509090426
42739CB00007B/533